How Do Our Ears Hear?

Carol Ballard

HODDER
Wayland

an imprint of Hodder Children's Books

How Our Bodies Work

How Do Our Eyes See?

How Do Our Ears Hear?

How Do We Taste and Smell?

How Do We Feel and Touch?

How Do We Think?

How Do We Move?

Editor: Ruth Raudsepp
Illustrators: Kevin Jones Associates and Michael Courtney
Designer: Phil Jackson

First published in Great Britain in 1997 by Wayland (Publishers) Ltd

Reprinted in 2001 by Hodder Wayland, an imprint of Hodder Children's Books

British Library Cataloguing in Publication Data
Ballard, Carol
How Do Our Ears Hear? – (How Our Bodies Work)
1. Ear –Juvenile literature 2. Hearing – Juvenile literature
I. Title II. Jones, K. III Courtney, M.
612.8'5

ISBN 0 7502 3465 2

Picture acknowledgements
The authors and publishers thank the following for use of their photographs:
Chapel Studios 5(top), 14, 16; Chris Fairclough Colour Library *cover*, 4, 23, 27;
Robert Harding 6, 10; Hearing Dogs For The Deaf 25; Popperfoto 29;
Teletec International 24; Zefa 5(bottom), 22, *contents page*.
The remaining pictures are from the Wayland Picture Library.

Typeset by Phil Jackson
Printed in Italy by G Canale & C. S. p. A.

Contents

Ears

Our ears are very important. We use them all the time to hear what is happening around us.

▲
We use our ears to listen to the sounds of the natural world. It would be strange if we could not hear the birds singing.

We hear many different types of sound. Some give warnings, like fire and smoke alarms. Some sounds give information, like the announcements at airports and railway stations, news bulletins and weather reports. Alarm clocks wake us up and telephones ring to let us know someone wants to talk to us.

We listen to the radio and television for pleasure. Although television has pictures, you do need the sound as well. Try watching your favourite television programme with the sound turned off and see what a difference it makes.

We use sound to communicate. We tell each other stories and jokes, and listen to each other's problems and secrets. This book will tell you more about your ears and how they work.

Our ears enable us to ▶ hear friends on the telephone.

5

Parts of the Ear

Each ear has three sections: the outer ear, the middle ear and the inner ear.

The outer ear consists of flaps on each side of your head called pinnae. They are made of cartilage, a stiff, bendy material, which is covered with a layer of skin. Each pinna acts like a funnel, channelling sounds into the ear.

◀ Elephants have enormous ear flaps to help keep them cool.

Look at your ear lobes in a mirror. Are they curved or flat? Look at your family and friends' ear lobes too.

The bottom part of each pinna is called the lobe. It is softer than the rest of the pinna because it does not have any cartilage inside. Some people have curved ear lobes while others have flat ear lobes. The shape of your ear lobe is passed down in families, in the same way as the colour of your eyes and hair.

The rest of the outer ear is a tube called the auditory canal. Sounds travel along this tube to reach the middle ear.

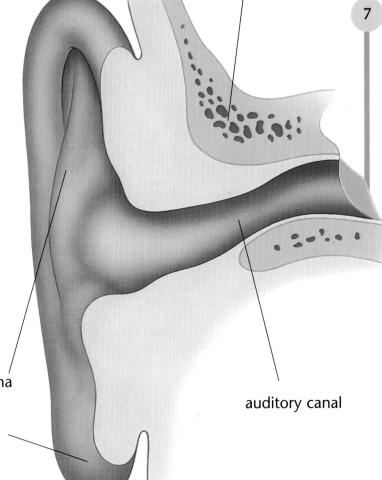

skull bone

pinna

auditory canal

ear lobe

The outer ear ▶

The Middle Ear

The middle ear is a tiny space filled with air. It is less than 20 mm high and 5 mm wide. It is separated from the outer ear by the eardrum.

The eardrum is a thin sheet of skin-like material. It is stretched across the end of the auditory canal and is attached to a ring of bone.

Sounds travel across the middle ear via the ossicles.

▼

hammer

the ossicles

anvil

stirrup

skull bone

eustachian tube

eardrum

space filled with air

Inside the middle ear are the three smallest bones in the body: the hammer, anvil and stirrup. Together, these are called the **ossicles**. They are linked together to form a chain of levers and are held in place by muscles and cords.

▲

Your ears pop in an aeroplane because the air pressure changes, and the eustachian tube opens with a 'pop' when you swallow.

9

The middle ear is linked to the space at the back of your nose by a tube. This tube is usually closed but air can pass through it when it opens. This keeps the **air pressure** inside the middle ear the same as the pressure outside.

The thin eardrum is stretched tight like ▶ the skin on the top of a drum.

The Inner Ear

The inner ear is a complicated network of spaces and tubes, all filled with liquid.

The inner ear is separated from the middle ear by the oval window and the round window. These are very thin sheets of skin-like material stretched tightly across two gaps in the skull bone. They keep the liquid inside the inner ear and keep air out.

▲
The inner ear is sometimes called the labyrinth because it is like a **maze** of tubes. The labyrinth was a complicated maze. According to Greek legends, a monster called the Minotaur lived at the centre of it.

◀ The spiral cochlea is rather like a snail's shell. It gets its name from the Greek word for snail, kokhlos.

The cochlea is a coiled, bony tube filled with liquid. It is lined with tiny hairs which play an important part in hearing. They are linked to the auditory nerve, which carries messages from your ear to your brain.

Also in your inner ear are three loops called semi-circular canals. They are attached to a sac called the utriculus. These do not help you to hear but they play an important part in keeping your body balanced.

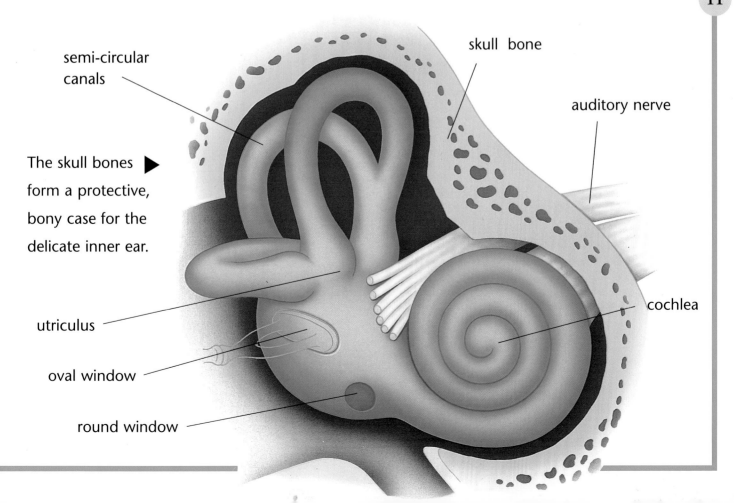

semi-circular canals

skull bone

auditory nerve

The skull bones ▶ form a protective, bony case for the delicate inner ear.

utriculus

oval window

round window

cochlea

How Do Ears Work?

A sound is a very tiny movement in the air, called a wave. To hear a **sound wave** it has to travel through your outer, middle and inner ear.

1. Your pinnae channel sound waves into your ears.

2. The sound wave travels along the auditory canal.

4. The vibrating eardrum makes the ossicles vibrate. The hammer hits the anvil, then the anvil hits the stirrup. The stirrup hits the oval window.

5. The oval window vibrates when the stirrup hits it.

6. When the oval window vibrates, the liquid in the inner ear vibrates.

7. The vibrations pass along to the cochlea.

8. The vibrations move the tiny hairs on the cochlea.

3. The eardrum **vibrates** when the sound wave hits it.

9. The hairs send messages along the auditory nerve to your brain. Your brain sorts the messages and you hear the sound.

10. The vibrations reach the round window. The vibrations gradually disappear.

13

Hearing Different Sounds

Think about some of the sounds you hear. Some, like birdsong, are high and others, like thunder, are low. How high or low a sound is we call its 'pitch'.

small wave pattern

large wave pattern

▲
Different sounds have different wave patterns. Loud sounds have larger waves than quiet sounds.

We can hear a wide range of pitch, but some sounds are too high or low for our ears to detect them. Some other animals can hear them – there are dog whistles that can be heard by dogs but not by humans.

◄ The thicker the string, the lower the sound it makes.

High-pitched sounds have waves very close together. Low-pitched sounds have waves further apart. The inner end of the cochlea responds to the close wave patterns of high notes. The outer end of the cochlea responds to the spread out wave patterns of low notes.

Loud sounds have larger waves than quiet sounds, so they make larger vibrations inside your ear. Messages from your cochlea to your brain tell it how big the vibration was, so your brain can work out how loud the sound is.

Do these instruments make high or low sounds? (A clue: the bigger the instrument, the lower the sounds it will make.) ▶

Loud and Soft

The loudness of a sound is called its **intensity**. It is measured in **decibels**. We cannot hear a sound quieter than 0 decibels: this is the 'threshold' of our hearing. Sounds can be quieter than 0 decibels, but our ears are not able to detect them.

Loud noises can damage our ears. People who use noisy equipment wear ear defenders to protect their ears. Loud music can damage our ears, too.

◀ This woman wears ear defenders to protect her ears from the noise of the machinery.

Find out about the noises around you by carrying out a sound survey. Choose your classroom, playground and street. At each place, stand still for five minutes. Record the sounds you hear on a tape recorder or on paper. (You might need to decide on a code or shorthand so it does not take too long.) Look at your results to see which was the quietest place and which was the noisiest place.

140 will damage ears
130
120
110 may damage ears
100
90
80 very loud
70
60
50 quiet
40
30
20
10 very quiet
0 threshold of hearing

decibels

▲
Record the sounds from your sound survey on a chart like this.

17

Balance

The three semi-circular canals and utriculus in the inner ear help the body to stay still when we are sitting or standing, and to balance when we are moving about.

▲

Travel sickness is caused by the brain receiving two different messages. The eyes tell the brain you are moving while the inner ears tell the brain you are still. To stop feeling sick, look ahead at the horizon so that your eyes will be still.

Inside each canal is a structure like a swing door. When you move your head, the liquid inside the canals pushes these doors open or shut. Tiny hairs inside the canals and utriculus detect this movement and send messages to your brain. The brain uses this information to work out the new position of your head.

Have you ever spun round and round and then felt dizzy when you stopped? The liquid inside the utriculus cannot stop as quickly as your head. It keeps moving for a few seconds so your brain still gets messages from it after you have stopped spinning.

Each canal lies in a different direction, up and down, right and left and back and front. ▼

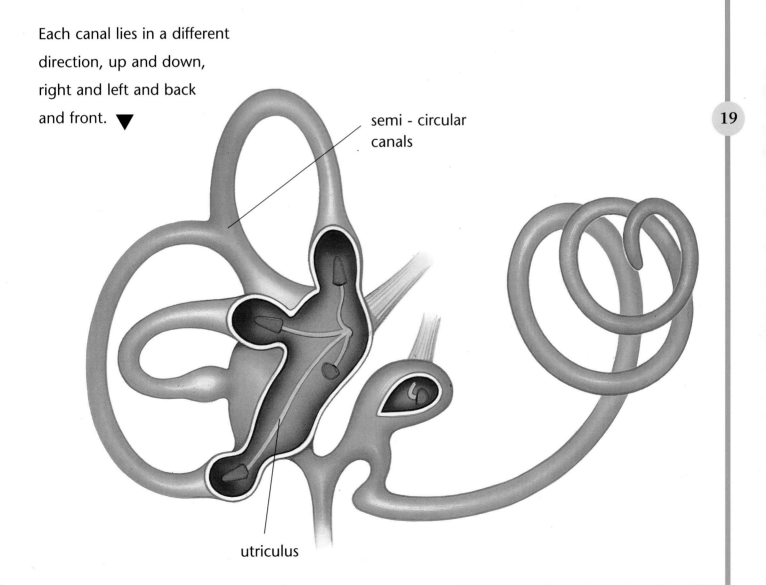

semi - circular
canals

utriculus

Using Two Ears

Have you ever wondered why you have two ears and why there is one on each side of your head?

▲

Some animals can move their ears independently of each other to help pinpoint exactly where a sound is coming from.

Having two ears helps tell the direction a sound has come from. A sound will reach one ear a fraction of a second before it reaches the other. It will also be a tiny amount louder in one ear than in the other. The brain puts together the information from both ears and works out where the sound came from.

Find the direction of a sound. Ask a friend to blindfold you and then to move a few steps away. Choose a noise, like clapping hands. Ask your friend to make this noise from different positions. Can you tell exactly where your friend is? Now repeat the test first with your left ear covered and then with your right ear covered. Can you still tell where your friend is?

These children are trying to ▶ find out whether two ears are better than one.

How Well Can You Hear?

Not being able to hear properly can cause problems with learning. Doctors and health visitors test how well babies and young children can hear, but unless the problems are serious they are often not noticed until a child starts school.

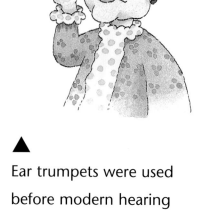

▲
Ear trumpets were used before modern hearing aids were invented. They acted as enormous pinnae, channelling more sound waves into the ear.

◀ A doctor may use a special audiometer to test a baby's hearing.

A hearing specialist will check whether the child can hear high and low sounds, and loud and quiet sounds. Then the specialist will try to find out why the child cannot hear properly. He or she will check to see whether the outer ear is blocked, and may also examine the eardrum using a special instrument called an otoscope. An otoscope also allows the middle ear to be seen. Any signs of infection or other problems can be detected.

Many people, as they get older, suffer gradual loss of hearing. They may decide to have a hearing aid fitted.

These girls are deaf so ▶ they use hearing aids and **sign language**.

Deafness

Deaf people need special help so that they can lead independent lives. Machines are designed to help deaf people do everyday activities. They may use a telephone with a printer to write what the caller says. A light may flash when somebody presses the doorbell. Deaf people may use hearing aids. These are tiny microphones that fit inside their ear and make sounds louder.

◀ The screen on this telephone lets a deaf person see what the caller is saying.

Some deaf people have 'hearing dogs'. These dogs are trained to alert their deaf owners to sounds such as the door bell, telephone and alarm clock. Instead of barking, the dog is taught to touch its owner and then lead them to the sound.

Many deaf people can understand what other people are saying by lip reading. They watch carefully as the person talks, and work out what is being said from the shapes and movements of their lips.

A hearing dog can help a deaf person to do things we take for granted. ▶

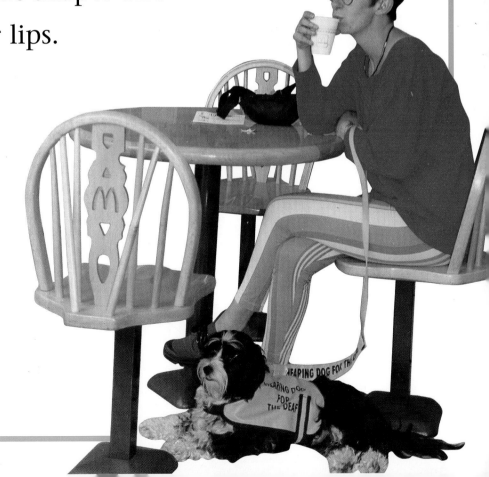

Sign Language

Many deaf people use **sign language** to help them to communicate with other people.

Sign language has been used for hundreds of years. In medieval monasteries, monks in 'silent orders' were not allowed to speak, so they used sign language to communicate with each other. There are still some monasteries like this today.

A

B

C

Here the first four ▶ letters of the finger alphabet can be seen.

D

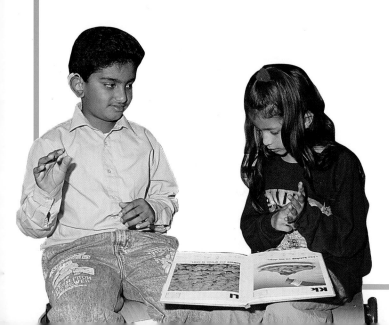

◀ These children are using sign language.

There are two types of sign, those for whole words and those for single letters. Words which are used a lot have their own sign. These are often **gestures** which we use naturally, like a shiver to say 'cold', 'thumbs up' to say 'OK', and shrugging shoulders to say 'I don't know'.

Words which are not used often do not have their own signs. Instead, they have to be spelt out one letter at a time, using an 'alphabet' of finger and hand positions.

Children who are born deaf often find it difficult to learn to talk. Their teacher uses sign language instead of talking to them.

▼

Look After Your Ears

It is important to look after your ears. Here are some suggestions about how to keep your ears healthy.

▲
You may enjoy loud music but it is not good for your ears.

Try to keep them clean and free from too much wax. Never stick anything inside your ear, it could get stuck.

Loud noises can damage your ears, so try to avoid them if you can. When listening to a compact disc player, make sure the volume is not too high. Try not to use earphones for long spells without a break. Avoid spending too much time in very noisy places.

If you take part in an activity where ear protection is provided, then make sure you use it.

If you have had problems with your ears, follow the advice of your doctor. You may have to stop activities like swimming for a while, but it is only for a short time and your ears have to last you a lifetime.

At large pop concerts and music festivals it can be very noisy. ▶

Glossary

air pressure The force of air pushing against something.

decibel The measure of how loud a sound is.

intensity The loudness of a sound.

gestures Movements of the hands, head or body to show feelings.

maze Paths and passages designed to puzzle those walking through them.

ossicles The three tiny bones in the middle ear.

sign language A system of gestures used by deaf people instead of speech.

sound wave The movement of sound through air.

vibrate To move backwards and forwards very quickly.

Books to Read

Funny Bones and Other Body Parts (How it Works series) by Anita Ganeri (Marshall Editions, 1996).

Hearing by Mandy Suhr and illustrated by Mike Gordon (Wayland, 1993).

Loud and Quiet (Start-Up Science series) by Jack Challoner (Belitha Press, 1996).

The Senses – Hearing (First Start series) by Lilian Wright (Watts, 1994).

Index